Before There Was Before

Poems

Wendy Drexler

Iris Press
Oak Ridge, Tennessee

Book Design: Robert B. Cumming, Jr.

Library of Congress Cataloging-in-Publication Data

Names: Drexler, Wendy, author.
Title: Before there was before : poems / Wendy Drexler.
Description: Oak Ridge, Tennessee : Iris Press, [2017]
Identifiers: LCCN 2017001599 | ISBN 9781604542394 (pbk. : alk. paper)
Classification: LCC PS3604.R4966 A6 2017 | DDC 811/.6—dc23
LC record available at https://lccn.loc.gov/2017001599

Acknowledgments

I am grateful to the following publications in which these poems first appeared, some under different titles, others in different forms:

Barrow Street: "The Life-Size Doll Made for Oskar Kokoschka" and "At His Last Dinner Party, François Mitterrand Eats Two Ortolans"

Big Ugly Review: "On Buying a Postcard of *Wheat Fields with Cypresses* by Van Gogh"

Blood Orange Review: "If There's Nothing" and "Praisesong"

Cider Press Review: "Epithalamium" and "Light R48 on the Storrow Drive Underpass"

Common Ground: "Before There Was Before," "A Cricket Has Been Calling," and "The Book of Apology"

Freshwater: "Adam and Eve"

Ibbetson Street: "Too Much or Not Enough"

JuxtaProse Literary Magazine: "At the National Archaeological Museum in Athens," "Apples Burning Like Small Suns," and "The Nine Fortunate Things"

Meatpaper: "The Birds of John J. Audubon"

Moon City Review: "Photo of Serbian Women, circa 1920"

Off the Coast: "Earth's Soliloquy," "Microbes," "Wild," and "Exhibit of Victorian Hummingbird Jewelry"

Pedestal: "Fate and Chance"

Poesy: "Out on the Plaza"

Prairie Schooner: "The Cave of Pech Merle"

Salamander: "Forbearance" and "Squirrel Eating the Milky Way"

South Florida Poetry Journal: "Relationship Theory"

The Comstock Review: "The Elephants"

The Hudson Review: "The Birch" and "Closing the Loop on the Year"

The Mid-American Review: "Beetle"

The Worcester Review: "The Pear Tree on Woodford Street"

Umbrella: A Journal of Poetry and Kindred Prose: "Still Life with Glasses and Tobacco"

Valparaiso Poetry Review: "Considering Paradise"

"Earth's Soliloquy" was featured on *Verse Daily*.
"Shelter in Place" was featured on wbur.org/cognoscenti.

"The Whole Spent World Comes Rushing Back" appeared in *Dead in Good Company,* edited by John Harrison and Kim Nagy, *Ziggy Owl Press,* 2015.

I am grateful to my children, Julia Baron and Noah Drexler Becker Baron, and my husband, Herbert D. Friedman, for their abiding love and support; to my friend and mentor Barbara Helfgott Hyett, who always advocates for the best writing in me and separates wheat from chaff; to my friends and gifted colleagues Suzanne Berger and Nancy Esposito, for reading my manuscript and offering essential comments and wise counsel; to Debi Milligan; to all the members of the Workshop for Publishing Poets, in which many of these poems were revised, for keeping the writing engines tuned and humming; to my Monday Morning Group, in which many of these poems came down the arm: Steven Ablon, Barbara Helfgott Hyett, Wendy Mnookin, Sarah Snyder, Connemara Wadsworth, and Allen West; to my poet sisters from Marie Howe's 2011 workshop at the Fine Arts Work Center, Provincetown: Jane Bachner, Cynthia Barger, Anna Birch, Lin Illingworth, Phyllis Katz, Kathy Nelson, Myrna Patterson, Marilyn Potter, and Vivian Eyre with special thanks to Vivian for the gift of writing time in her Long Island studio; to Eric Hyett and Dalia Geffen, for smart edits; to my Monday-night poetry friends: Rob Arnold, Michael Mack, Tam Neville, Myrna Patterson, Diane Provost, Bert Stern, and Anna Warrock; and to Martha Collins, Nick Flynn, and Marie Howe, whose workshops at the Fine Arts Work Center have invigorated my work.

I also would like to express my deep thanks to Robert and Beto Cumming for selecting my manuscript and for their steadfast support in bringing it to life.

Contents

I

II

III

If there's nothing here but atoms…

—Carl Sagan

✧

All actual life is encounter.

—Martin Buber

I

Before There Was Before

1

Before there was before, there was still before,
no verb to carry the abyss.

Light from dark, this from that, an easing
of boundaries, a slit
making a run for it,

everything
blue at the edge of that pose.

2

The Big Bang hurled all the star stuff
ever to be made—brazen tumult,
lashed by the muscle of spume,

hydrogen and helium waiting
for their rings to close,

dark tonnage, billions and billions
of mewling seed stars,

all burning and burning
themselves out, the universe
braced to decay.

3

The shoulder of one boulder settling
against the shoulder of another.

Canyons cleaving, granite
wrenched free.

The apple asleep
inside the sleeping tree.

4

The tide slinks in.
Shelves of blue-green algae.

Bluefish.
Lungfish.
Weakfish.

5

Shaggy-maned mushrooms
sink and dissolve. Beneath,
beetles frill.

Pea vines, holdfast clovers.
Bees shiver the white throats.

6

Whales slip through the slot.
Baleen and blue milk spilled
through all the rooms of the ocean.

Long lives call and click
the grievous migrations.

Sharp-shinned hawks seize
their trophies, clamping down
the whole lid of air.

7

When trees come, they are meant to
be climbed.

Stay away, or come, or come
just this far—you and I are
here, the compound of us,
a colossal conjunction.

And the calendulas in the field
who are riddled
with life-spark and flaws.

Let's take a stab
at the dark, let's
time our tea,

if we have tea,
if we have time.

If There's Nothing

Did Monet love light more
than he loved Rouen Cathedral, or did he
need to stand
long enough in the same place to see

that nothing stays, even
evening is eroding, the saints
in the portal of the cathedral
softening in each other's gaze.

Even the dead refuse
to stay dead: and so Cerberus needed three heads
to keep the dead
from leaving the shadow kingdom.

Yesterday, the pond was dazzled by the turquoise wings
of dragonflies mating midair,
the water lilies helixing—
everywhere I look is a pool of sensation.

And in the morning, my brain begins
to savor the coffee
before my hand reaches the cup.

Let's touch it all. Call it home.

Microbes

And because of microbes, I write faster,

scribbling, no time to take time

by the bridle, no catching that mane

flung back over the distance, flick-flicking.

One hundred trillion microbes call us home,

and so we morning glow, newborns ride

the birth slide, arrive coated with an amazing carnival of enzymes.

Settle down now. Success is just

killing us. Keep going then, and may the clouds

of your breath spell out

what words take too long to explain.

Earth's Soliloquy

Forgive me if I feel a little shaky.
In 7.59 billion years, the sun
will drag me from my orbit, turn me

to cinder for all Time. No infinity
to buttress the fragile, finite measure
of a human life, a mere threescore and ten.

No more clinging to the gospel
of the flowers, the sun never going down.
Oh, my amplitude of tides. My fists

of rubies and diamonds, canyons
and amaranth and oaks. Let me slip
through the slot of drought

and melt. Yet even I
am to be spun sugar. When all this Time
I'd thought I was for keeps.

Necessity

Evolution dealt us
a good hand—
predatory eyes,
an opposable thumb,
a savvy heart
to secure a share.
The white lotus of lungs,
the brainstem swaying
like cel grass, the fetus
in the womb, chafing,
compressed, propelled
in spasms—human,
blessed, and cursed—
all of us together
in the same room,
everythingcomingcloser,
not understanding that we are
all of us together
in the same room.

The Cave of Pech Merle

— Cabrerets, France

They mixed their paint in their mouths,

spat paint from their mouths, onto the walls—

out came manganese mammoths,

red ochre aurochs, bison stampeding.

And drew two spotted horses, one behind the other,

stepping down. The stone wall

makes a place for a shoulder, for a jaw,

that horse come rippling through the wall.

And around them, a nimbus

of six stenciled human hands, fingers spread wide.

Palms pressed down hard.

And pregnant women and an outline of a man impaled

by four long, painted spears.

He's naked, red as meat on a spit, and his eyes are embers.

His mouth a grimace of falling—

25,000 years of falling from the edge of where we begin.

I'm Reading Darwin

1

On a tiny rocky island in the Atlantic,
a few months out on the *Beagle,* Darwin found
only two kinds of birds, the booby and the noddy,

both... of a tame and stupid disposition,
easily distracted and deceived—the males
couldn't stop crabs from snatching

the flying fish they'd left near the nests
for their females. They even let
those crabs steal their chicks.

And on that island, not one plant,
not one lichen, no royal palms succeeded
by majestic plumage, succeeded

by Adam and Eve's descendants.
Instead, just two dumb birds,
on whose feathers and skin and shit

the life of the island hinged; and a species
of fly that lived on the booby; and a tick
burrowed in noddy flesh; and a small brown moth

that fed on the feathers; and a beetle
and a woodlouse that fed on dung;
and a host of spiders, who fed on them all.

2

In Santa Fe, Argentina, Darwin said, a man splits
a bean, places the moistened bean on his
sore head, and his headache goes away.

A broken leg? Kill and cut open
two puppies, tie them on either side of the leg.
Replace doubt with a plaster!

Did Darwin despair? Or still believe
in a God who would break our chains?
On a dark night, south of the Plata,

he comforted himself with the sea's
most beautiful spectacle... every part
of the surface... glowed with a pale light...

two billows of liquid phosphorus
before the ship's bows, *and in her wake...*
a milky train.

Adam and Eve

He came down to the sea.
She came up from the sea,

their bodies not yet credible,
not yet dry. They are still

just clay, silica, sea
and sea bed, weathered rock.

Words are broth
and their tongues ladles—

How will they ford
the blue-green world,

bear the heaviness of hips,
their busy breath?

Sand will be scratching
their skin, the scorching

sun easing into dusk.
Under their hot tent of stars,

date nuts, sweetmeats, pearls of fire.
Artichokes with wings.

Hard things: eight winds
and sixteen quarter-winds.

Slow things: ennui, eternity.
Fast things: pillars of salt,

quakes, hunger setting
a torch to the world.

Considering Paradise

—after a needlepoint by Lydia Hart, 1744, Museum of Fine Arts, Boston

Adam's curly ringlets, Eve's embossed
brown hair sewn halfway to her waist.

Paradise is petit-point, cross-stitch and trellis, thistle,
Tudor roses brimming over the strawberry border

bound by thousands of ambitions. Solid blue,
that sky above the tree, the two, the view

of low-hanging fruit, the double-cross-
stitched snake. The pair stare straight out, hands braced

on hips. Her lips, costly coral. The garden teems—
a butterfly, a brown yarn worm. A snail who dreams,

spiraling, and chain-stitched beneath the creatures' feet:
Adam and Eve in Paradice that was their pedigree....

Greed decided. Adam's fig leaf already basted into place.
Eve's breasts held high. Her nipples, two French knots.

Praisesong

Night-quartered are the sheep.
The sorrowful sheep, paired

in skyless stalls, dark pens,
singled out: the chosen.

Did they pool
their separate languages

into a grammar of contraction?
Who curried favor, who grew

dominant, who stepped on toes,
who couldn't, or wouldn't,

or didn't? Who got angry
and kicked a stall? Who

was lulled by hospitality
and daily feeding, until

the stalls in the Ark swung open,
and they tramped together

two by two down the ramp.
And the pine needles clinked

bright coins of dew.
And the robins blazed,

plumped themselves up a little,
jounced in the puddles, shaking out

their wings and calling
to each other in quick tongues.

Fate and Chance

Round and round spins the compass
rose, madly on its wheel,

as Fate and Chance fight
over who has more:

Fate claims the long view.

Chance holds fast to living,
intuition, improvisation.

Fate shouts: *But I have the Second Coming*
coming.

Chance replies, *I can be there*
at a moment's notice,

straddling
the fault line.

Fate freezes the sky
until it weeps.

Chance bears down
on fields burned black with famine.

Our cheeks pale.

We seal
our lips.

Everyone pays the price.

At the National Archaeological Museum in Athens

Pity the dead
children found in
a grave in Mycenae.
Gold leaf where
there were fingers.
Gold leaf
rolled into hoops
for earrings.
Gold leaf,
slit to leave
open the eyes.
Gold leaf
over the brows,
over the knobs
of the knees,
their feet.

Out on the Plaza

Men sit cross-legged on the sidewalk
trying to sell neon balls made in China—
smiley tomatoes, oranges, squishy lemons.

They throw them down for us—see how
they bounce back up for 1 euro.

For 75 euros, I can buy a coin purse
made from the skin of a stingray,
the clasp embedded
with that ray's white tail.

Farm-raised in Italy, the man says.
Waterproof, the man says.

The eye needs something to lean on.

History Repeating

—after Pomegranate, *a film by the Israeli artist Ori Gersht*

A pomegranate, רימון,
hangs motionless against a black screen
set in a wooden frame.

Offside, a bullet slithers in
slow-motion, slams into flesh,

splattering the hive of seeds
that bursts—רימון!
The fruit flaps from its noose.

Juice spurts on the leaves
of green cabbage dangling

from its own string. A rain of rind
and pulp falls on the cucumber
that juts out over the edge of the frame.

A wedge of cantaloupe faces out,
trompe l'oeil, shimmering—

someone's sweet breakfast—
as the seeds of the pomegranate
glitter cold as rubies, falling, falling.

Rimon, same word:
pomegranate, grenade.

From the other side of the wall,
I watch the LCD screen darken, reloop:
the bullet slithers in again.

Nazi Photograph

The prisoners have just stepped off
the train. Terezín. In the crowd, a little boy in shorts.
His favorites? His only?

Bare legs, dirty knees. A tin cup dangles
from the boy's neck. Maybe his father tied it there
with a shoelace.

His jacket sleeves swallow his wrists.
A coat button or the place where one is missing.

The camp begins where the tracks run out,
where a prisoner conducts

Verdi's *Requiem* on a legless piano,
the prisoner chorus singing the Latin by rote—

> *Dies illa solvet saeclum in favilla.*
> That day dissolves the age to ash.

The singers and soloists are deported
to Auschwitz. The conductor,
Raphael Schächter, is deported to Auschwitz.

> *Libera animas de profundo lacu.*
> Free the souls from the deep lake.

> *Libera eas de ore leonis.*
> From the mouth of the lion.

Archangel

—after a sculpture by Leonard Baskin

Is he among the righteous,
descended into the field
of human commerce

never to rise on those wings
with their tonnage of woe?

He has closed his eyes,
no words engraved
upon his tongue.

Bolted to the ground
in bronze armor, he is waging
witness, manacled to the Fall.

To be smithy and the forge,
hammered like that:
all excess
and overflowing sorrow.

His last labor is being
forced to hold the bountiful
world like a seashell to his ear—

The Life-Size Doll Made for Oskar Kokoschka

Will she be able to open her mouth? Does she have teeth and a tongue?
I would be overjoyed...
—Oskar Kokoschka

After Alma Mahler left him, the artist sent
the doll maker his oil sketch drawn from memory—
the swale of her spine, tracery of ribs,

her ears, pink as a harbor at dawn,
all the shores of his obsession. Inspected
and returned a model of the head,

with revisions: trim the chestnut rigging
of her hair, widen the bezels of her eyes.
When his Alma doll arrived, he clasped

her cloth hands in his, kissed the sawdust
of her swanskin breasts. They wouldn't warm.
He took her to bed, felt beneath her

blue silk jacket, her lisle slip, posed her
upright in a chair, or déshabillé
in a low-cut dress on the sofa,

painted her with a rabbit on a red cushion,
with a dog, with a doll on the same red.
Her last night, he partied her, had his servant

parade her in black lace before his guests
to the strains of a string quartet, champagne—
at dawn, Kokoschka drank the last

of a bottle of Burgundy, smashed the glass
against a wall, slashed her neck with a shard,
the wool batting seeping red,

the selvage of her throat unraveling.

Apples Burning Like Small Suns

1

Cézanne damns the paint for being paint
and damns himself for his faith in its lies—

chrome yellow to suspend the lemon
over the edge of the table's hard swill,

Verona green to balance the pitcher
perilously still. And who is indentured

and whose black knife splices one thing
from another, espaliered like doubt?

And what is
softly hammered into sacrifice?

What perfection?
What private courtesy?

His coat is stiff with quarry dust,
obedient to the peg.

2

He paints the apples to burn
like small suns, strokes them
into the bright infinitudes.

He chisels two peaches to a fine pink point,
until they are ready to caress,
intimate as a hand on a thigh.

3

He cannot tame the river
stones and grass. He tips them
with violet until they leer.

Three skulls simmer in their sheds.
First, they roar. Then silence.

4

The long green stems of onions beg
a thousand small decisions,
how to clench the air, how to let go.

The mirror and the green olive jar
are equally generous.

The white tablecloth hurls itself up
like the stiff peak of Mt. Sainte-Victoire.

The puce mushrooms are too terrible—
how little they live. Only

his vermilion pears are loyal.

5

The Dutch iris, the peony,
the rose madder tulips

live with such conviction, despite
the mutiny of dying.

They break his heart—*Flowers!*
he writes, *I've had enough.*

II

Photo of Serbian Women, circa 1920

Four women glare right through the lens.
Against the sun, against the wind.
Unsmiling, barefooted, wearing babushkas

and dirndls over long, dirt-stained skirts.
One of them holds a bundle in the crook of her arm
from which an infant's tiny leg, skinny as a dowel,

dangles, accompanying her mother into the field
or from the field. Potatoes? I want something
from that field. Under another woman's apron,

a goat or sheep, and in her right hand, a bucket.
In her left hand, an ax. And what does it matter now,
this pause in the road, these four women,

the infant, long dead, and how little
I'll ever know—stories etched in breath—
my assimilated Jewish grandmother Millie,

a French Levy, whose sapphire and diamond
bracelet I wore to my wedding. My grandfather
Sam, a socialist, born in East Germany,

who always said he was from Russia
to side with the peasants. He cut a door
in his warehouse for stray cats, wore

a suit and silk vest to feed the squirrels
in Denver City Park. Named the squirrels after
his grandchildren: Marian, Richard, Wendy.

They always came when he called. When I was born,
the doctor told him he had a granddaughter.
He told the doctor, *Please look again*—

All These Years

The leaves are damp, moldering,

resigned to unbecoming—

rudderless, the reds, ambers scabbed with blight.

Dew on the birch drains into dirt.

Branches lie where they've fallen,

bark peeled raw, the tree unhinging.

Haven't I been careless, expecting better,

or more, or something else, aren't I always trying

to strip the sky bare?

Closing the Loop on the Year

Snow clings to shingles. I riffle December
pages of my calendar—coffee-stained days,
bills paid, to-dos and past dues,

the late tracery of time spent, nearly
forgotten. I peel
the cellophane from the new calendar, turn

the blank pages. I want another year, *oh yes.*
And another after that. I want
tenacity like the dogwood outside my window,

preparing to stay, bare branches huddled hard
against the side of the house—
the one shoot that races straight up

from the middle of the crown—
brown umbel with its parasol of stalks,
each stalk capped with a pink bud

ready to be struck into white stars,
on whose account, by May,
the whole branch will tremble.

The Book of Apology

Some things I don't profess to understand.
—Stanley Kunitz

The last time I saw my mother I was reading
on the patio, when she came out,

cinching her bathrobe around her,
her wrists thin as a wren's,

her arms, slack saplings. Her belly, swollen.
Blue veins trawled her pale face.

She asked me if she could sit beside me.
Yes, I told her. And she said to me,

Wendy, I want you to know I've had a good life.
I think it was the first naked thing she'd ever said.

✧

I didn't really want to understand
that she had just opened the door

the dying must pass through to leave us.
And what did I do or say to her then?

I might have muttered something, or nothing.
Or did I bow my head, and return

to my book to find my lost place?

✧

She took the long bus ride.
Traveled all day and all

night to get there. No ticket, nothing
to place in the overhead bin.

When the bus pulled up to the station,
she had nothing to declare.

Shadows unfurled. She stood there
in the glaze and sipped the light.

Her dying was slow. I didn't hold her.
We weren't like that.

The Elephants

This is their poetry, their grief.

Slowly they sway
the gentle stamens of their trunks.

One wraps her trunk around
her mother's skull.

One combs his mother's pelvis
with the sole of his foot.

The cheeks of the elephants are matted
with red grass and stained with tears.

The elephants flap the ruffled flowers
of their ears.

They have found her bones.
There's nothing left but bones.

Chameleon

I wore him to my mother's house.
My father bought him for me,
with that little collar and little leash

around his neck, pinned to my sweater
where he clung. All he'd need:
a glass tank, some plants for when

he wanted green, a rock for turning brown,
a jelly lid for water. He slept beside my bed.
I'd run home from school, grab him

by his tail, let him run along my arm.
His little feet were dry as pebbles.
He wanted down, so I let him

scamper across my bed, but he disappeared
beneath the sheets. When I called out
Mom, she made me leave my room,

shut my door, hide with her in her room
down the hall. The two of us lay down
on her bed, pulled the covers up

to our necks behind her closed door—
my own chameleon, who was so quiet,
so camouflaged, lying there in wait.

The Birch

I scramble up the slippery trunk. I'm five,
in my own backyard. I fling my one leg,
then the other, hoist myself into the tree.

Then I crack open the shells
of my sunflower seeds, wiggle out
the kernels with the tip of my tongue,

spit the empty shells down to the grass.
I peel bark the way I want to,
the way I peel my scabs to see

the pink skin, the new part underneath,
just born. I watch
clouds scrub the sky. I stay up here

in my brave room until all the fathers
have walked home from the bus stop after work,
carrying the newspapers under their arms,

the streetlights just coming on.
My father is not coming home. He's left
my mother and me and all

his shirts and his camel's hair coat
in the hall closet. All his books
on the shelves, even my favorite

with the little brown dog I love
on the cover, his front and back legs
outstretched, running hard.

Forbearance

The cows look slowly up,
flick flies with their tails,
with their ears, the whole
of their flanks twitching
like wind through wheat.
They stamp their feet,
shrug their shoulders,
come close to the wire,
walk away. Their heads
are warm and swarming.
Damnation of flies
they bear stoically. Maybe
they are burning up inside.
Maybe they want to jump
out of their hides.

Too Much or Not Enough

—*after Hopper's* Nighthawks

I study a matchbook.
Count the matches.
How many strikes have I got left?

The waiter bends to his small tasks.
A man in a booth with a blue suit orders
eggs over easy. He could be my father.

I leave my coffee cup on the counter.
Outside, I kick a stone into the gutter.
The street yaws.

O, catch me, Father; catch me,
Mother, before what came
between you comes between you.

Here are the lips of me, the hips of me,
the sill and will of me,
the whorls of my serious ears.

Too much or not enough has been said.
It may never be morning.

Relationship Theory

Each spring, long-legged waders
flock to Florida to nest in trees
above alligator-infested swamps.

Clouds of them, full of industry,
festoon every branch: storks clack
their bills in courtship, an egret

warms her eggs. Grass and twigs
brim from a heron's bill. Below,
alligators nose the muck, rustle up,

shake the trees to topple nests.
Jaws gobble any chicks that fall out—
and keep other predators away.

Hard to tell, exactly, if protection
always comes at such a price, or if
juggling intimacy with brinksmanship

is love. And what did I know,
when I married young,
perched out on the end of a pliant and precarious branch?

What I'm Keeping

I'm keeping my ex-husband's handmade love
letters from 1969 in their burlap bag

in the closet under the front stairs.
Red construction-paper cards, paled to pink.

My mother's sweaters, the dressy dove-gray
cashmere with the sequined sleeves, and how

I told her with certainty, smugly,
before I knew she was dying,

that I *definitely wasn't* going to have any children.
I'm keeping my guilt, streaming through me

like sunlight strafing a window.

The Fly

He loves my coffee mug, buzzes above it,
        hovers, lands on the lip, sidles inside,
that fly I'm pretty sure was the one I saw
        fucking another fly on the ceiling
last night. Now my mother's in my ear, *flies*
        carry disease, so I cover the top
of my mug with the poem I've been writing
        before getting up to dampen
a paper towel, wipe his germs from the lip.
        I'm sorry I've had to
use vulgar language in discussing the fly,
        who is now my fly, I suppose,
and who is leaving me and my mug alone
        for the time being. Admittedly, I've tried
to kill him more than once because of his
        devotion to me and my coffee,
his curiosity, full-throttled, his drone-barreling
        dart and swoop, his lust for touch.
Blazing, brimming! And the two of us smack dab
        in the middle of this very room,
with work to be done, getting away with
        this one-and-only fitful, little, lucky life.

My Granddaughter, Soon-to-Be Born

Imagine you, adored, basking
in the speed of the F train

to Brooklyn—its grit, and all
the shoes sheathing the subway floor—

black boots, leather-tongued,
red canvas sneakers, pointy-toed

cowgirl boots like the ones I used to wear—

squeal of air brakes, tang of stale beer.
Out the window, the quilt of a blue sky.

And I, who will wheel you past
every stranger, every danger,

my guardian voice skimming
the air between us.

Wandering in the Community Garden

I've come because one plot is all for beauty—
zinnias, daylilies, a flamboyant fleet
of marigolds that won't last past frost.

I've come for sunflowers nodding
their heavy heads—proof that exuberance
has its own logic, its own reward.

I've come to devote myself
to the sprawling tapestry of vines,
and to Brussels sprouts climbing

their spindly-necked stalks. I've come
to hear the dark-green collards chime,
to count the butterflies—

cabbage whites—climbing the ladders
of the sun. And to feel the earth, for this
slow hour, breathe easy in its bed.

Listening to a Schubert Cello Sonata

I started crying two bars into the Allegro moderato—
the ice I'd been carrying, melting away.

Crying because the cellist was making love
with his bow, playing the score

with his whole face, raising his eyebrows
when a phrase ascended, puckering

his lips at a dissonant passage, jerking
his head to one side for emphasis,

half smiling, then scowling lightly.
And I was crying for the intimacy

of their conversation, without the bickering
that even two people who love each other

can't help but do. And because
the pianist and cellist knew

what the music wanted—they hovered
slightly, let the last note waft into silence—

brief bloom emptied, as if into a wound.

A Cricket Has Been Calling

As I wash my cereal bowl,
my blue coffee cup,
as I fill the feeder, a cricket
has been calling. I listen
for some inflection, an iamb,
I am, I am, any pattern or meaning,
but there is none, or nearly none—
just the scrape of wings, emphatic,
vaguely duple time, insistent, tireless.
Or else a pause, and I think, *ah then,*
something is settled, for once.
But the cricket resumes,
an engine unrequited, an equation
to be solved, growing large
as a sound can grow—and I think
of the woman crying at the bus stop
this morning, and her children,
grieving for their father,
who is never coming back,
and I wish I could find a place
for that cricket to rest,
a place to rest
for everyone who calls and shakes
and has not been consoled.

At Dunkin' Donuts

A man and a woman are talking close.
He crumbles a muffin, takes a bite,

bows his head over the Styrofoam cup
he's cradling in both hands, palms it

side to side, gouges the lip
with his thumbnail. Her red sweater

glows like sunrise as she leans her head
on his shoulder, smooths his forearm

with the tips of her fingers, combs a crumb
from his sleeve with the side of her hand,

brushing away each undone, every undeliverable.
And I want to pour them a pitcher

of blue sky, plant an apple tree between their arms,
save his cup for my Museum-of-What-

Makes-Us-Human, the wear and tear of it,
the coffee-stained too-muchness of it,

that brush of touch that caresses an arm,
a shoulder. That grace, that brace, that balm.

At Mount Auburn Cemetery

We've come for the trees
and for the willow pond,

for the dogwood, the weeping
beech and the dell filled

with birdsong. We've come
to choose our gravesite.

I pick up a maple leaf.
Each vein, a river of ladders.

Wind riffles the unfallen.
We read gravestones—the infants,

and the long lived I envy,
until I remind myself they're dead.

We debate motifs—
sheaves of wheat,

winged skulls, an urn half draped,
an urn laid bare. We stroll

the perennial borders arm in arm
to the iron Gate.

On Buying a Postcard of *Wheat Field with Cypresses* by Van Gogh

At Saint-Paul de Mausole,
Van Gogh weeps and washes

his brushes with the tip
of his tongue, and with his tears.

In his fields, cicadas clench him
like fever. He paints

olive trees that toss like silver
spoons inside a drawer.

He paints the fields carmine,
smears viridian on the flames of cypress.

Clouds, a yellow sky,
sullen hooves of mountains.

The Pear Tree on Woodford Street

Obstinate bud, sticky with life, mad for the rain again.
—Stanley Kunitz

It was the poet who dug

deep the hole in dirt

the way his mother told him.

And here it stands, blossoming

a hundred and one years,

light-deprived, hemmed by houses

and the gnarl of winter char. And smog.

and moth, and maggot.

And those leaves will reluster as they rise

to bear the bright brocade of pears

plump in their green-gold cambering.

And the sun.

Still Life with Glasses and Tobacco

—after a painting by Willem Claesz, 1633

Walnuts and their splintered shells,
rot on a lemon, a swale of stains

cut to pith and peel, a silver compote

tipped sideways on the table,
two smoking pipes, just snuffed,

smoke spiraling. Three olives shine.

A silver bowl, also shining.

Everything basted in glaze,
and in the goblet's curve,

the artist has painted himself
held at bay by the halter of the real.

Wild

Turkey, rough, and brawling,
sopping wet among wild roses
equally out of season.

Where are your woodland, your acorns,
your oak mast,
your rapture of ants?

All night you forage by the backdoor trash,
and in the morning, I drive past you
as you strut into traffic, straddling
the yellow line on Concord Avenue,

dividing everyone
coming
from everyone going.

Light R48 on the Storrow Drive Underpass

Praise the beam of that light that slices
through late afternoon traffic.

and the faint scatter of that light
on the roadbed graded to a gradual bend.

Praise the gradual bend.

And praise the worker who climbed
up the catwalk at 4 a.m. to tape

the stencil, R48, high on the tunnel wall,
spray-painting *R48* in rusty red,

and then mounted the back plate,
connecting the cable to the power source,
completing what is

every day taken for granted, among all
the hours, perishable, yet to come.

Shelter in Place

—April 19, 2013

And Boston is a dark harbor,
hardened, the streets furrowed
with chase, with grief, and a marathon
of turns—hairpin, wrong—
and dead ends, a desert
of dead ends without provision
or cure. Tanks and sirens stampede
all day, all of us at home
behind locked doors mining
the TV screen for every last look,
the price everyone will have to pay,
and a man climbs out of a tarp-covered boat
in someone's backyard, a rifle's
red laser dot locked on his head,
a blood skew crazing his face
as he raises his bloody hand,
his bloody shirt, to show he is unarmed,
while just a few blocks away
from that very yard, two shelves
nailed to a tree, paperbacks on top,
hardbacks below, and a sign—
Take a Book, Leave a Book—
and as the city raged that day, all day,
the Little Free Library stayed open.

Epithalamium

—for Julia and Robert

I want to give you a poem with a pond in it,
and if you see a heron glide down

to fold the blue smocking of her wings,
swishing silence, remember her
when you stand at the edge of things.

There are blueberries to ripen over you,
orioles to weave their pure paired notes of song,

tadpoles to skim and flex their tails
the color of bark and rain.

And if a willow topples into the pond,
welcome the host of ants and aphids
who'll tunnel through.

Forgive what others might call
fallen, or lost. Turtles will clamber up

from hard winter, bronze on their backs,
to doze in repose beside each other on warm stones.

Be with each other as gentle as that.

Hydrangeas

Pour themselves over the fence

like buckets of sun-blazed cream.

I brush a fleshy petal, wondering how

the branches can bear them, the way the blossoms

thrust aside the leaves in their impatience to descend,

all bustle and pomp like the girls

who snubbed me in high school.

Yet when the light drains into dusk,

the blossoms ease into a watery-blue

tenderness, willing to slur boundaries,

blend into branch, blend into bush.

Becoming devotion. And look,

already they are wilting a little—they will keep on

wilting, there will be no stopping them.

More gently now than before,

I brush two petals

with the tips of my fingers to lend courage

as they tuck themselves back in—

they, too, not yet entirely lost in the darkness.

Love Poem for My Husband

We're celebrating our new patio
furniture, the striped cushions

that pick up the warm tones
of the acacia-wood table and chairs,

the new umbrella, a Special Order
from Bed Bath & Beyond—more

than enough shade! We pour
two glasses of wine, drink

the late-afternoon slant light, savor
the clouds as soft as lambskin,

the table oiled to a sheen. You say
we should plant a lilac tree at the bend

in the road so we won't see
the traffic. I tell you that the fox

urine I bought at the hardware store
and sprinkled on the flower bed

hasn't stopped the rabbits
from snapping off the daisies.

I get up to rip out some swallow-wort
before it strangles the forsythia, and think

of the dead who have nothing
to do, while we fret in the garden,

take another sip of Malbec,
nibble goat cheese on a cracker, letting

the good enough be.

III

The Nine Fortunate Things

—after a Korean watercolor

And the waterfall has turned
into white curling ribbons.

Rocks are fortunate to be
the same deep currency as trees

that fling open green sleeves,
releasing an ibis to dip

his bill into sunrise.
Among the fortunate

glossary of stars,
dazzle of cobalt and rain.

In a bed of grass soft enough
to listen, the wind.

Two red mountains,
their shoulders above clouds,

wear the scent
of feathers.

The Birds of John J. Audubon

1

It was the custom to nab one of every kind—
parakeets flexing on boughs
of cocklebur, the great blue heron,

the chalice of its throat, palm warblers
fluttering in blossoms, the ivory-billed
woodpecker, still strapped to air.

Before their colors faded in that first hour,
Audubon chose the best specimens,
inserted wires through sinew and scute

and wing, espaliered carcasses
in arabesque, demi détourné, and passé
on pegboard, posed in flight or forage.

He took up his paints—filled their eyes
with the blue of another world.
Then he roasted them. Wasting nothing,

he ate them, praising, above all,
the flesh of the green-winged teal, flush
with wild oats from Green Bay.

2

Snow geese, too trusting, and so many,
it didn't seem to matter: he bagged
a hundred a day from the sky.

He nabbed a basket
of Carolina parakeets,
just two shots.

Passenger pigeons, a dot
in his notebook for each

passing flock—163 dots
in 21 minutes—a cloud of dots,

a roaring gale that took
all day to pass.

3

He shot the Arctic tern
in sufficient numbers to finish
his picture from life—noting

his *curious experiment,*
the three times he shot a female
and threw her body out on the water

to watch the male land on her
and try to caress her.

At the Pavilion of Nature

—Jardins de Marqueyssac, Vézac, France

A taxidermied fox snags
with a paw a taxidermied pheasant,
red on his moth-eaten snout,
mouth contorted into snarl.

Not a diorama, more
like a slaughterhouse:
thrushes, linnets, hoopoes,
and grebes pinned behind glass,

slathered with painted blood.
Four inches above, three owls
gape at the gouged-open
breasts of the songbirds.

I flinch at the carnage,
look away, notice the plaster-
spackled forest floor, count
invertebrates: two snails,

dried in the grass, one black-
backed whirligig beetle,
one yellow swallowtail, fallen,
a century dead below the fray.

Exhibit of Victorian Hummingbird Jewelry

What is more soothing than the pretty hummer?
—Keats

For the widow's black silk shoulder,
one hummingbird was murdered,

preserved with arsenic, burnt alum,
and tanner's bark,
packed into a gold brooch.

Gold sheaves of leaves for wings.

The eyes? Studded cold with rubies.

Two more birds were killed
for earrings.

Necks, slit.

The tiny gold flared toes.
The rufous crowns, spiked stiff.

The breast of one is green fluorescence.
The other fades to olive near the mouth.

No more nectar-lapping tongue
or frenzied hum, no splendor-surge,

no more mind that savored
wild scarlet sage.

O, pretty hummers, how
your gold stiletto beaks dazzle,

how you shriek.

At His Last Dinner Party, François Mitterrand Eats Two Ortolans

—Latche, France, New Year's Eve, 1995

Tiny ortolans, skylarks, served sizzling pale
in yellow fat. Mitterrand took one whole bird

inside his mouth (its endangered olive green
and yellow, its dash of ruby trapped

in the French Ardennes
wheeling its way to Morocco).

Inside his mouth with only
the legs sticking out.

Alouette, gentille alouette, / Alouette, je te plumerai.
Lark, nice lark. Lark, I will pluck you.

The bird blinded, plucked,
stuffed with millet, grapes, figs,

drowned in Armagnac. He took it
inside his mouth, and bit

into the lungs and stomach,
savoring the burst of brandy

(*ortolan* from *hortus, horticulture, garden*),
the tiny bones of the head sweet as hazelnuts.

Morphine-drugged, eight days
before he died, the President of France

covered his own bony, brilliant head
with a damask napkin to concentrate

the aroma, crunched another whole bird,
then leaned back, ecstatic.

At the Rumfish Restaurant

Everyone wants to dine beside the giant fish tank
that covers the back wall.

I ask the waitress if the coral's real. No, she laughs.
The fish circle the artificial reef,
cycling in the bubble of coexistence—

the tank glows, the fish as lulled as I am—
no adrenal rush pumped through neurons
in the engineered hush—

yellow-tailed lookdowns, slim as quarters, skim past,
and placid black drums,
their serious, whiskered chins.

A moray eel slithers by, loosening
the four-foot green belt of himself.

I order grouper, watch a grouper
hover under a fake rock as I cut and chew,
gagging on grouper flesh, awash

in cognitive dissonance. Time to let
the tide propose something new.

Harbor

The flock hunkers down,

as compact as little tanks,

battened down along brown flanks,

yellow beaks like lamps turned down

low all night in the harbor,

somebody's target, somebody's

opportunity, or regret—black ducks

treading hard to stay

in place, rising and falling

and rising again

in the chop.

Beetle

His black-shellacked body
lay belly up on the basement floor,
everything in him already

decided, the huge husk of him—
three sections knuckle-coupled
like train cars: the abdomen scribed

with scarabs, compact as a flower bulb,
the thorax hinged to his tiny head,
and inside that, the minuscule brain

that mounted his little music, day
and night issued meek and fierce
instructions to himself in his dark city.

And refused what? And raced where?
Sought what solace scuttling?
And did he notice or not the tepid light

squinting through smeared windows?
Did he brace his legs against the spin
of the washer's thrum? Nothing more

for him but this one hard look—to memorize
the six matched dancers of his legs,
each curving toward its partner in a series

of jointed etceteras all the way out
to the hooks, barbed, and beyond,
the ardent tips that almost touch.

Squirrel Eating the Milky Way

Hunched over a candy wrapper, a squirrel

holds the Milky Way between paws like a man clutching

a bottle in a brown paper bag, head bobbing,

short jerks and bursts, the whole body pressed

into service, front paws twitching,

tail flicking, rotating the crimped and crumpled paper,

attending to the labor with the ardency

of ancestors who crossed the Eurasian shelf, rustling

the rip wider to extrude the gooey constellation,

inhaling every particle—saturated, caffeinated, partially

hydrogenated, and artificially enhanced—

intoxicated by the halo of globular clusters, all the dark matter.

A Dead Carp

Only the wedge of the head
is left, floating on its side.
Not floating, exactly,
more like listing in the shallow
salt marsh. Mouth open,

as if gasping, still suffering
the loss of the body—jaws open, too,
and the lips, pursed and swollen.

One upward-staring eye,
hectored and hapless,
and over the whole face
a caul shredding into wisps like curtain sheers
with each shift of scattered light.

And in that dissolution, the singular head
gleams like the shield of Achilles.

Fiddler Crabs

Fallujah is on the news.
The bay draws back into itself,
strummed by cold light,

rucked with mud,
shrapnel of shells.

Crabs scuttle sideways,
simmering,
a pulse of nerves.

They shake their fists
They run.

The sun sharpens its spine.
The whole coast, out in front.

Flock of Glossy Ibis

Driven by light, by season,

and supply, they winnow

salt-marsh grass, slim fringe of coastline—

plunging down-turned bills

into mud-brine and tide-crease,

plucking crabs, snails, caddis flies.

Plumed in brightest gloss

for breeding, chestnut breasts

ebb into the gorgeous oily incandescence

that cannot be purchased, cannot be owned.

They wheel above me, a blaze of hurry—

The Whole Spent World Comes Rushing Back

The great blue heron bends low,

her legs a long and silent shear. Underwater,

the shadow of vigilance flexes.

In the broth of silt and moldering leaves,

she clamps a frog in her bill, shakes it

from side to side,

her feathers a handkerchief fluttering.

From the cave of her mouth, the frog flails, kicks,

flashing white, the belly refusing to surrender,

everything at stake in the long stretch and gape.

Notes

P. 21-22 Italicized text from *Charles Darwin, A Naturalist's Voyage Round the World: The Voyage of the Beagle*. New York: Skyhorse Publishing, 2014.

P. 29 רימון is the Hebrew word *rimon,* meaning both "pomegranate" and "grenade."

P. 30 Romanian pianist, composer, and conductor Rafael Schächter performed Verdi's *Requiem* at least sixteen times at Terezín. The final performance was for senior Nazi officials and a visiting delegation of the International Red Cross, sent to inspect the camp. Performing a Catholic Mass sent a coded message that the Nazis would be damned in the final judgment. Italicized text and translation of Verdi's *Requiem Mass* by Arthur Shippee, 2004, www.mendelssohnchoir.com. The photograph is from the Holocaust Museum, Washington, DC.

P. 32 Epigraph from the paper "The Artist's Inspiration: Alma Mahler's Influence on Kokoschka's Work," Jane Larson, March 2, 2006, carleton.edu/departments/gmrs/vienna/Kokoschka-Mahler.doc.

P. 35 *Flowers! I've had enough!* is from Cézanne's letter to the poet Joachim Gasquet, in *Atelier de Cézanne,* by Michel Fraisset. Editions aux arts etc., English version, n.d.

P. 39 *Photo of Serbian Women, circa 1920,* Circa Now Gallery, Amherst, Massachusetts.

P. 59 The house at 4 Woodford Street in Worcester, Massachusetts, was the childhood home of Stanley Kunitz.

P. 63 The Little Free Library in Watertown, Massachusetts, was just a few blocks from the backyard where marathon bomber Dzhokhar Tsarnaev was found hiding in a boat.

P. 75 Hummingbirds beat their wings so quickly that they appear to be standing still. During the Victorian era, they were thought to "stop time," and widows wore jewelry made of their bodies as a symbol of mourning.

—Debi Milligan

Wendy Drexler is the author of *Western Motel* (Turning Point, 2012) and the chapbook *Drive-Ins, Gas Stations, the Bright Motels* (Pudding House, 2007). Her first children's book, *Buzz, Ruby, and Their City Chicks,* coauthored with Joan Fleiss Kaplan, was published by Ziggy Owl Press in 2016. Her poems have appeared in *Barrow Street, Blood Orange Review, Ibbetson Street, Nimrod, Off the Coast, Prairie Schooner, Salamander, The Mid-American Review, The Hudson Review, The Worcester Review, Valparaiso Poetry Review,* and other journals; featured on *Verse Daily* and WBUR's *Cognoscenti;* and in the anthologies *Blood to Remember: American Poets on the Holocaust* and *Burning Bright: Passager Celebrates 21 Years.* She has been both a poetry editor and a cavity-nest monitor for the Massachusetts Audubon Society. A three-time Pushcart Prize nominee, she is a native of Denver, Colorado, and lives in Belmont, Massachusetts, with her husband.

CPSIA information can be obtained
at www.ICGtesting.com
Printed in the USA
BVHW03s1733050318
509716BV00005B/975/P